SCHOLASTIC

TRUE OR FALSE

AMPHIBIANS

BY MELVIN AND GILDA BERGER

All amphibians live on land and in water.

TRUE OR FALSE?

TRUE! Amphibians are animals that generally spend their lives part in water and part on land.

Almost all are born in lakes, ponds, or streams. As adults, most amphibians leave the water to live at least some of their lives on land. Some continue to live near water. Others settle in places far from water. But most return to water to lay eggs.

The word *amphibian* comes from the Greek wor amphibios, which means "living a double life."

Frogs and
toads are
the most
common
amphibians.

TRUE
OR
FALSE?

TRUE! Frogs and toads make up the largest group of amphibians.

These two kinds of animals are very similar, but there are some differences. A frog's skin is smooth and wet, but the skin of a toad is dry and bumpy. Also, most toads are chubbier than frogs, and many toads live far from water.

Frogs and toads make up nearly 90 percent of all amphibian species.

Toads jump like frogs do.

TRUE OR FALSE?

FALSE! Toads cannot jump nearly as well as frogs can.

In fact, toads rarely jump at all. Most of the time, they walk on their very short legs. When attacked, frogs usually use their long, powerful hind legs to leap away. Toads sometimes use their hind feet to bury themselves in the ground to avoid predators.

Most toads make their homes in gardens, fields, forests, and jungles.

Brightly colored frogs are usually poisonous.

TRUE OR FALSE?

TRUE! All brightly colored frogs have poison glands in their skin.

Any predator that tries to bite one gets a mouthful of bad-tasting liquid. Sometimes one bite is just enough to make a predator let go of the frog. Other times the poison is actually strong enough to kill the attacker. The tiny poison dart frog is one of the most dangerous of all amphibians.

Some South American Indians hunt with arrows dipped in frog poison.

FALSE! Many frogs and toads blend in with their surroundings, making them hard to see.

Their skin is natural colors like green or brown, just like their environment. This camouflage often makes it easy to hide from snakes, their worst enemies. It also helps them catch crickets, worms, and other animals they like to eat.

Most frogs and toads grow a new skin every few weeks — and then eat the old one!

All frogs and
toads call
and croak.

TRUE
OR
FALSE?

FALSE! Only male frogs and toads (and a few females) call and croak.

This happens mainly in mating season. The males gather in ponds, swamps, and other wetlands. They puff out their throats and force air over their vocal cords to make the sounds. The females hear the males calling. They find them, mate, and lay their eggs.

Bullfrogs make a deep sound — jug-o-rum, jug-o-rum.

Frogs and toads lay many eggs at a time in water.

TRUE OR FALSE?

TRUE! Most female frogs and toads lay lots of eggs at a time in water.

Generally, they lay the eggs and swim away. However, some carry them on their backs for safety. The water keeps the eggs from drying out. The eggs, which do not have shells, are covered with a jelly that protects them.

Large clumps of eggs stuck togethe are called frog spaw

Fully formed
frogs hatch
from eggs.

TRUE
OR
FALSE?

FALSE! Generally, larvae hatch from the eggs.

The larvae are called tadpoles or polliwogs. They have small heads and long tails — and look nothing like their parents. For some other species, however, tiny froglets hatch from the eggs.

Tadpoles breathe underwate through gills.

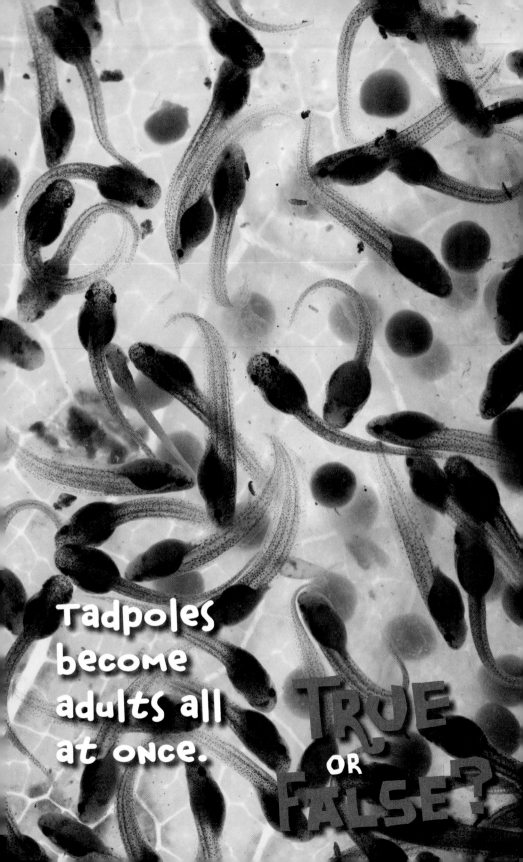

Tadpoles become adults all at once.

TRUE OR FALSE?

FALSE! Tadpoles can take up to five years to change into adults, although most reach adulthood within three months.

As the larvae develop and become larger, they grow hind and front legs and lose their tails. At the same time, the larvae develop lungs so that they can breathe air. Now they're finally ready to live on land as adults and have young of their own.

Larvae usually eat algae, while adults usually eat insects

Frogs and toads sit in the sun to keep warm. **TRUE** or **FALSE?**

TRUE! Sitting in the sun helps frogs and toads warm up.

That is because frogs, toads, and all other amphibians are cold-blooded. Their bodies stay at about the same temperature as their surroundings. If the weather gets too cold, the animals are not able to move around. In winter, many go to sleep in holes they dig in the ground.

Some amphibians take a long summer nap when conditions get too hot and dry.

Most frogs
and toads
are small.

TRUE
OR
FALSE?

TRUE! Frogs and toads are generally smaller than most fish, birds, or mammals.

An average frog or toad can fit on the palm of your hand. One of the smallest frogs is the Brazilian gold frog. This tiny creature is only about as long as a housefly and weighs less than a Ping-Pong ball!

Little grass frogs are the smallest Nort[h] American frogs.

Salamanders are lizards.

TRUE OR FALSE?

FALSE! Salamanders are amphibians; lizards are reptiles.

The two kinds of animals are sometimes confused because they look similar. But here's how you can tell them apart. Most salamanders have moist, smooth skin and short toes, and they lay their eggs in water. Most lizards are dry and scaly, have claws on their long toes, and lay eggs on land.

Most salamanders have four toes on each front foot and five toes on each back foot.

All salamanders have tails.

TRUE OR **FALSE?**

TRUE! Salamanders have very unusual tails.

If a salamander loses its tail, it grows back! Sometimes a predator—like a snake, owl, or turtle—grabs hold of the amphibian's tail. To escape, the salamander drops its tail and runs away. In time, the salamander grows another tail that's as good as new!

Adult salamanders can take from abou` one to three month to grow a new tail.

All salamanders are small.

TRUE OR FALSE?

FALSE! The biggest salamander — and biggest amphibian of all — is almost twice the size of a toddler!

The salamander that holds this amazing record is the Chinese giant salamander. When fully grown, it can be as long as 6 feet (1.8 meters) from the tip of its nose to the end of its tail. Chinese giant salamanders spend all their time in the water.

Chinese giant salamanders find pre[y] by smell and touch not sight.

Salamanders are most active during the day.

TRUE OR FALSE?

FALSE! Salamanders usually stay out of sight during the day.

They spend the daylight hours hiding in rotten logs, among fallen leaves, under rocks, or in similar places. These cool, dark, humid hiding places keep the salamanders moist and safe from enemies.

Spring is the time of the year when you're most likely to see salamanders.

Salamanders are fussy eaters.

TRUE OR FALSE?

FALSE! Most salamanders will eat just about anything they can catch.

Their main diet includes insects, spiders, and worms. When food is hard to find, salamanders can go for a long time without eating. The tiger salamander is one of the biggest eaters. When hungry, it will even eat other salamanders.

Salamanders have sticky tongues for catching food.

Newts are salamanders.

TRUE OR FALSE?

TRUE! Newts are a kind of salamander.

They have tails, like other salamanders do, but theirs are flatter. Their skin is also often drier and bumpier. Some female newts lay eggs one at a time on plant leaves under the water. They use their feet to wrap a leaf around each egg. The young hatch from the eggs and return to the water. Some, called efts, live on land before going back to water.

Wrapping eggs keeps them safe from predators.

A mudpuppy is a large salamander.

TRUE OR FALSE?

TRUE!

Mudpuppies are large salamanders that are found in Mississippi, Georgia, and other parts of the United States and Canada. Most live in freshwater ponds, streams, lakes, and rivers. They swim among water plants, eating small animals and fish eggs. Mudpuppies are active at night and in winter, too.

Mudpuppies keep their featherlike gills all their lives

Caecilians are worms. TRUE OR FALSE?

FALSE! Caecilians look like large earthworms, but they are actually amphibians.

Caecilians have the same smooth, moist skin as most other amphibians. Most live in tunnels that they dig in the ground. A caecilian uses its strong, pointed head to dig itself quickly into the soft earth.

Caecilians have mouths full of sharp, needlelike teeth.

Caecilians live only in the tropics. **TRUE OR FALSE?**

TRUE! Caecilians are found only in hot, tropical places.

They are rarely seen because they generally live under the ground. Their eyes are tiny, or covered with skin or bone, and almost invisible. Their senses of smell and touch help them get food, find mates, and avoid being eaten.

Tiny feelers below each eye help caecilians touch and smell.

Many amphibians
are endangered.

TRUE
OR
FALSE?

TRUE! Many kinds of amphibians are having trouble laying their eggs and raising young today.

By cutting down forests, draining swamps, and building houses and roads, humans are destroying the places where amphibians live. Oil, pollution, and acid rain are spoiling the clean water that amphibians need to survive.

Nearly one-third of all kinds of amphibia are in danger of disappearing.

It's too late to save the amphibians. TRUE OR FALSE?

FALSE! There's still time to save endangered amphibians.

Experts are studying the problem. Many adults and kids work to clean up the land and water where amphibians live. Governments pass laws to save the amphibians' habitats. Some set aside protected areas where amphibians can make their homes, find mates, lay eggs, and grow in number.

More amphibian species are endangered than any other animal group.

Index